An Indrawn Breath

Also by Gillian Telford, published by Ginninderra Press
Moments of Perfect Poise

Gillian Telford

An Indrawn Breath

PICARO PRESS

Acknowledgements

I am grateful to the editors of the following journals and anthologies in which some of these poems have appeared, often in slightly different forms: *Australian Poetry Journal*; *Famous Reporter*; *Five Bells*; *Island*; *Mascara Literary Review*; *The Canberra Times*; *The Night Road* (Newcastle Poetry Prize Anthology, Hunter Writers Centre, 2009); *Australian Poetry* Members Anthologies, 2012–2014; *A Slow Combusting Hymn* (the Hunter–Newcastle Poetry Project, 2014); *The Way to the Well*, Central Coast Poets 2014 Henry Kendall Award Anthology; *Out of Place* (forthcoming from Spineless Wonders); *Falling & Flying*, anthology (forthcoming from Brandl & Schlesinger).

The poem 'Vigilance' was a finalist in the Hunter Writers Centre *In the Detail* competition 2010; 'Before Rain – with Purkinje effect' was featured as poem of the week on the *Australian Poetry* website August 2012; 'The Music Tower' was highly commended in the *All Poetry Competition*, 2012; 'Dry-Spell' was poem of the month on the *Australian Poetry* website November 2014.

This manuscript was completed with the assistance of Varuna, The Writers' House, Katoomba, NSW, through a 2014 Publisher Introduction Program Fellowship.

I would like to extend my sincere thanks to Rob Riel at Picaro Press, to Varuna CEO Jansis O'Hanlan, and especially to my consultant, Deborah Westbury, for her unfailing support and encouragement.

To all my friends in poetry: the Central Coast Poets, the 'Focus' group, and the Pomegranates, my love and thanks.

An Indrawn Breath
ISBN 978 1 921691 76 8
Copyright © text Gillian Telford 2015
Cover image from the painting *Rockfall at Python Pool*
by Robyn Bellamy, 2015

First published by Picaro Press 2015

This edition published 2015 by
Picaro Press – an imprint of
GINNINDERRA PRESS
PO Box 3461 Port Adelaide 5015 Australia
www.ginninderrapress.com.au

Contents

1   9

roadworks	11
before rain – with Purkinje effect	19
autumn 2009, day 1	20
displacement	22
nominal rights	24
listen	25
after autumn	26
now breathe	27
trekking	29
tasting the day	30
about time	31
archetype	34
leaving	35

2   37

from Venice	39
family business	45
chiaroscuro	46
dancing figure	47
redhead (bathing) 1889	48
torso, 1954	49
Eingana, 1968	51
forensic	53
vigilance	56
a weight of hair	57
the music tower	58
flying blind	60
dry spell	61

3	**63**
the Green Room	65
pile high the platter – the mint is free	66
funambulism	67
the gift	68
levitation with LBD	70
sliced lime	71
quiet carriage	72
shock waves	73
Lord Howe Island	75
spectral horizon	76
gliding the Glories	79
a re-write	81
sound bite	82
pendulous wattle	83
well-bred	84
the third bridge	86
beyond my mother's garden	87
new day	90

i.m.

Evelyn Margaret Carmody (née Hodges)
07.03.1912–14.06.2013

William Edward Henry Telford
28.01.1907–24.12.1982

1

'the god of poets has two hands:
the dextrous, the sinister.'
– Margaret Atwood

roadworks

'Warning drums have ended all travel.' – Tu Fu (712–770)

'Perseverance furthers. It furthers one to have somewhere to go.' – The I Ching

(i) overtaking lane ahead

We drove north, that year
        looking for your childhood
searching for those summers
you wanted me to share.

        Caloundra
        Mooloolaba
        Maroochydore

the names rolled off your tongue
        easy   relaxed
        like your hands on the wheel.

But nowhere was the same   no beach
wild enough
        no campsite unmarred
No Fishing signs barring favourite wharves
        tomorrow
you'd show me the way that it was.

In time, you grew churlish
        implied it must be me
me with my migrant eyes
squinting doubt.
Yet still we drove

until we reached the point
of no return   beyond
the end of memories.
> And when we stopped

released at last to move
> through the heat, the ocean

and each afternoon's languor
it was all easy   relaxed
> like your hands

on the sweet, white crab-meat.

(ii) no stopping or turning

above the river the road
is sandstone-carved against sky
as blue as the eyes of Buddha

in the valley below
the freeway becomes lost
but found again   rising

like the perfect ending
from a kingdom of fog –
out of this grey silence

white lights swim upwards
monstrous shapes loom
then burst into sunlight

descending fast   three lanes
of brake lights and tail lights
glint red and vanish

she has some knowledge
of what lies ahead
      how the unimaginable
can rear up before you
scarlet-mouthed and leering
      how the most familiar

can become unknown
      she hasn't yet learned
how the damp cold

stiffens a spine
or how long it will take
to climb back into light

(iii) stop – wrong way – go back

it's always around the next bend
      half-seen, offering clues
           but never enough
it's always over the next rise
      smelling of fish, blowing its horn
           but moving too fast
it's always trying to catch you up
      wearing stilettos, asthmatic wheeze
           but ill-prepared
it's always around the next bend
      (it's always there)

(iv) slow vehicles keep left

They called it a fresh start
but it was their last chance

so they sold up and drove south
towing a caravan. Behind them

everything had doubled; debts
and children, resentments and half-truths.

Some they left on a sigh of relief
with the worst of the wedding presents,

the parents' red plush sofa.
Others, were left on an indrawn breath –

a swing beneath the jacaranda,
curtains at a nursery window.

And so much that went with them
they thought they'd left behind

until it came to light
       like moth-holed blankets,

silverfish through bookshelves,
the quiet work of years.

(v) night roadworks – expect delays

Behind me, strapped safe in sleep, the children sigh. I'm off-duty; off-guard. Lulled by silence and the headlights' probe, I can let the night stream by. And there are no more tears to catch me unawares, it's almost over. Ahead, the skyline glows – eerie, sulphurous. Speed signs blink by the roadside and warn from overhead: now lanes are merged: three then two then one: *prepare to stop*. We're waved to a standstill by faceless men whose bodies gleam and flicker at the road's dark edge. Behind them, night is thrown into unreal day like an open-cut mine on a lightning flash. Above me, helmeted figures swing in buckets from yellow cranes which prowl the sandstone cut. I turn to the children, limp and pallid in the halogen glare, and pray they'll stay asleep. We're moved on again; guided by more flashing lights and arrows past the swarming men, bulldozers and sheds, the banks of lights aimed at the sky. Back in darkness, I listen for the children; they stir but are not roused. We've come a long way.

(vi) no pedestrians, bicycles, animals, beyond this point

you cruise the streets in the old red car
shouting hallelujah
you walk fast through the park
by the river   round the mall
the quadrant   the race track
the library
you sit on a wall in winter sun
spooning butter from muffins   froth from coffee
you circle the fountain
repeat three times
go back the other way
repeat three times
you close the door
turn out the light
lie in the silence and examine
the miraculous space in your head

(vii) end – freeway

before me on the road
       tumbleweed
spins and drifts
lifts on the wind
       is gone

signal of loss
       symbol of transience

or a little girl's skirt
as she twirls in the breeze

(viii) steep gradient

It's open country here.
        The basalt slopes
long felled of cedar   cleared and grazed
seem to roll together with voluptuous ease.

You nod to an oncoming driver
then take your turn
to cross the one-lane bridge   river
surging dark below.

The green-rimmed valley
falls away   it's wilder country now.
You wind down the windows
        turn off the music
and sing the new air.

Now you're climbing
        every bend a stimulant
each look back
        a release
and from great stands of trees
the birds urge you on.

(ix) unsealed road

A ritual is complete
        the household gods appeased.
You turn a dial and Classic FM *Drive*
shifts your day down to *andante*.

Evening moves over the skylight
with flurries of twigs and leaves.
The lamps are lit
and every surface gleams.

This is where contentment hides
        waiting for the quiet hour
when each small task
assumes the guise of sacrament.

But all at once the tempo changes
        slides into tango   intricate
smouldering   leads you down back-lanes
you'd left far behind

opens up road-maps
at unmarked pages
        and then comes the rush
of discontent

you're back on the highway
thumbing a ride.

before rain – with Purkinje effect

In a strange half-light, the rain
is holding back,   the sun's only presence
a cloud-filtered glare.

Now the forest reveals its camouflage;
blotched and spotted, like a family of giraffes,
the tree trunks reach into foliage.

Rocky outcrops rise from gloom
into high relief, each moss-furred crevice
green as a mythical Ireland.

Along the gully, an updraught
lifts and splays the fingered palms
falls away, leaves them trembling;

and like tumbling clowns sent in for our
distraction, a flock of parrots riots
through the canopy. As swiftly as they came

they flee, scarlet plumage flaunting deeper red
against the sky. But before the light
drains from the landscape or branches

are bowed by rain, there is that moment
when all we can see is the exultant
surge of green.

Wikipaedia: the Purkinje effect (sometimes called *dark adaptation*…)
introduces a difference in colour contrast under different levels of
illumination

autumn 2009, day 1

The seasons slip
together here
 their changes
blurred and worn
as Hawkesbury sandstone.

Over the bay
early mist draws back
 a shoulder of headland
shrugs
then fades.

A small boat works
its nets. A distant figure
walks a dog.
A woman steps out
of a white linen robe.

But why aren't I ready
for this imperceptible slide
 that clean-rinsed sand
the single
morning swimmer?

In the far north
the beaker of the Gulf
has tipped
and spread its floods
across the grey horizon.

To the south,
the fires, like hounds of hell
outrun, outwit.
    Nothing
is pure white
or rinsed clean.

displacement

(i)

From the incoming tide
I rescue a stone
      deep olive green
tinged with yellow buff.

The colours bring echoes
of old growth forest, as though lifted
from leaf-litter, moss and fungi;
but stranded here

among the pastel shells,
the bleached and silvered grit,
it's a misfit
dumped on a tidal surge.

I roll it in my palm, turn
and stroke it with my thumb,
rub away each grain of sand
and hold it till it warms.

(ii)

In waves of harassment, the hostile
natives dive and shriek.
      From the fig's leafy head,
crouched in defiance, a red-eyed

intruder, huge and pale, keeps
them at bay with great snaps
of its bill and raucous cries.
When we're talking of birds

it's a summer migrant with many names;
stormbird or fig-hawk, rainbird or hornbill,
      a channel-billed cuckoo, flown south
to breed and find hosts for its eggs.

As I watch it struggle against the flock
I think of the journeys
across the ocean, grey wings beating,
hour upon hour;

driven by instinct and drawn
to our plenty,
each year they find refuge
despite the clamour.

(iii)

Across the Timor Sea, the boats
      keep coming.
Some we hear about, some we don't –

some will wait quietly, others won't.

nominal rights

A report from Christmas Island leaves a sense of shame –
families, still confined, still denied basic rights, and
children, in our care, now quoting numbers for their names.

Their drawings show grief no language can explain;
with fear of guards, of bars, of storms that rise at night.
Yet we say *Go away,* further cause for shame.

We forced through laws to save live cattle being maimed;
we beg release for chickens, huddled under lights
while children behind wire learn numbers for their names.

When compassion is withheld, when secrecy's ordained,
compliance is insidious, a mindset we must fight,
not wait for more reports, too late to halt the shame.

Each year, we bow our heads to silently proclaim
respect for those who fought for freedom as a right.
Some turn wrists, still scarred with numbers, not their names.

Our leaders are elected, we all must share the blame
but when we throw off apathy, democracy ignites.
A report from Christmas Island must be cause for shame
when children in detention think a number is their name.

ABC Radio National 24.3.2014: Professor Gillian Triggs, President,
Human Rights Commission, reporting on Australian immigration
detention facility on Christmas Island

listen

it's raining again
        on a gusting southerly

forest percussion
        on a steel-drum roof

wire brushes shifting
        through scatters of leaves

tapping of sticks
        against the glass

rattling gumnuts
        like shaking maracas

overfilled gutters
        playing a riff

a branch thuds down
        with a foot-slamming bass

somewhere a night-bird
        chimes a celeste

after autumn

after the sun no longer reaches above the ridgeline
    after the south face of the mountain darkens and is still

after the birds shift their morning Glorias to the far side of the bay
    the cries   faint memories of summer

after you climb the wooded slope
    where ferns and bracken lift and float
to bundle up great piles of storm-tossed kindling

after you carry your load inside
    eyes streaming tears of eucalypt and resin
fashion a nest of twigs and paper   strike a match
    watch the first flames spread

after logs are added
    then come murmuring voices
riffs of laughter   random jazz
    small sounds
like pages turning wood-ash shifting

the slow steady burn of winter

now breathe

sit on your chair, close your eyes, rest your left hand in your right hand, the receptive position / *as soon as we left the plane, I could feel the altitude settle on my chest* / let the soles of your feet feel the floor; now look into your mind, be aware of what you're bringing with you today / *Jomsom's nearly 500 metres higher than Mt Kosciusko* / breathe in through your nostrils then out through your nostrils / *and that was only the start* / in through your nostrils and smell the air / *loose shale and boulders, not hard but always climbing* / if your thoughts are wandering bring them back to your breath / *I was already breathing hard* / now check your face, make your face soft; your eyes, your nose, make them soft, soften your mouth / *thought I wasn't fit enough* / check your body, soften your buttocks, find your feet, your legs / *we trekked all morning, through and beside the Kali Gandaki river-bed, winter-dry* / your spine; soften your shoulders; / *saw clouds of dust become herds of goats, whistling boys* / find any tension and breathe / *the Annapurnas overwhelming the sky, the snow-gods* / in through your nose and out through your nose / *I was a struggling mite* / now breathe in / *a mote in a moonscape* / turn your head to look over your left shoulder, hold it there / *what had happened to our short first day* / exhale your head back to centre; breathe in / *we reached Kagbeni but no room at the inn* / now look over your right shoulder, hold it there / *so our sherpa moved us on* / and breathe out a long slow exhalation / *now I was really in trouble* / breathe in as you return your head to centre; / *he had to pace me* / on the exhalation bring your chin down to your chest, hold it there / *little-steps-little-steps, stop, hands on your waist, gulp for air, little-steps-little-steps, stop* / and breathe / *so high now, looking back, how far we'd climbed* / exhale as you lift your head / *balloons of lungs sucking thin air* / back up to centre / *would they collapse* / To join me now and seal today's practice / *it started to snow, to get dark* / take your hands up to the third eye centre / *the others in trouble too* / to acknowledge your mindfulness / *all of us little-steps-little-steps, stop and breathe* / your intuition / *crawled in to Jharkot, snow drifts building* / close your eyes, breathe in deeply / *Tibetan lodge, charcoal braziers under the table, hot garlic soup* / and on the exhale join together in humming ommm / *had we found nirvana?* / thank you everybody for your energy today; Namaste.

trekking

behind me   whistles and hoarse cries
the bell sounds of ponies

before us
where the track had plunged
     now a washout
water seeping from the mountain
     pooling on the stony shelf

the porters kept moving
     steady and sure   the only way

i had to go on

behind me   whistles and hoarse cries
the boys   urging the laden ponies
     panniers bulging   swaying
and weaving   down the mountain
     the bells coming closer

i had to go on

if four-footed ponies could find
     safe passage
well so could i

and if i stopped here
     they would keep moving
steady and sure   the only way

tasting the day

for Pat

sometimes it's important
that each day tastes the same

sometimes it's important
as the porridge warms your tongue
that each day tastes the same

sometimes it's important
as the porridge warms your tongue
the tea steams in sweetness
that each day tastes the same

sometimes it's important
as the porridge warms your tongue
      the tea steams in sweetness
the marmalade is bitter
that each day tastes the same

sometimes it's important
as the porridge warms your tongue
      the tea steams in sweetness
          the marmalade is bitter
to remember the days
that didn't taste the same

about time

(i)

I'd promised I'd knock-off early and then I got mad with her because she'd forgotten the blinds again. I told her real country women knew how to handle a heatwave. She said she was under the impression that real country men took their hats off when they came inside so why didn't I go and have a cold shower and wash off all that muck instead of whingeing at her. She was right of course. After I got cleaned up, I came back to the kitchen to check the mail and wait for a cuppa but she came up behind me, threw a towel across my shoulders, pushed down hard with both hands and said *Don't move*. And before I know it, she's combing my hair, first with her fingers and then that scratchy old comb. It felt pretty good until she started going on and on about *time; never enough time, no time for each other, making time*, and all the while she's combing and snipping and grumbling with the scissors flying so wild I feared for my ears. Then all of a sudden she stopped – went very quiet – flicked off the towel. She was still behind me though. I could feel my neck prickling but I didn't move, I didn't say a word. I just stayed there until I felt her hands on my shoulders again, pressing so hard with her thumbs I had to drop my head. Then she moves in closer, bends over me and starts blowing away the hair – with little breaths and pauses – breaths and pauses. And she was right of course. It was about time.

(ii)

Thin flakes of skin
        fall like ash

crusted sun spots
weep and craze

there's a hat-line
stamped
across your brow
        I tuck a towel

around your shoulders
        you bow your head
as though in submission
        or is it a flinch of remembered touch?

I lift and open
the sharp old scissors
        my other hand finds
the first strands of hair

I comb and cut
        feather and shape
        try not to touch
your pallid skin

for then something rises
tight in my throat
        I must look away
drag down a breath

slumped in the chair you're
        childlike   grateful
I lift off the towel
and shake it outside

        the midday sun
is fierce on my arms
I watch the hairs drifting
        light as down

alone inside   you call me
you call me
but I have left you
and made my way back

to hot afternoons
        the way it was then –
when we'd pull down the blinds
and I'd cut your hair

archetype

their heads find the earth
like truffle hounds, searching

    their feet, set wide
with a squaring of rumps

their knuckles are swollen
in fingers of patience

that move through the soil
with the rhythm of seasons

they're all the old neighbours
we've passed in their gardens

    all the old women
we've watched from a train

they're the black-clad wives
lifting potatoes

the brown-seamed villagers
sifting through stone

they bend from the waist
but make no obeisance

they live by the wisdom
they've stored in their joints

and when you reach down
to show me a flower

for the first time I see
that's the way you now bend

leaving

I lift pictures from walls, wrap them
in sheets, pack them in blankets.

Outside a lyrebird calls and splits
the air, darts across a sandstone shelf;

somewhere in my mind, I meet
its searching eye. I strip the bookshelves,

topple rows of babies, brides and gilt-
edged smiles. Cupboards empty, boxes fill,

my future starts to totter. Now mirrors stand
and face the walls, old rugs are rolled

and tied. Across the polished floor, light
finds tracks of cars, of trains, the years

of tiny wheels. I hear the she-oaks brush
the roof, a turkey work the forest floor

and as I slow my broom, another fall of leaves
comes tumbling from the rough-barked gum.

2

'Symbols
   are a poem's endearment
they murmur
   and suck one's ear.'
      Dorothy Porter

from Venice

'The promise of travel releases essences
and glazes everything with Expectations' – Gail Jones

(i) *pavimento alla veneziana*

The terrazzo floor
of this seventeenth century mansion
slopes
like a lesson on perspective
towards the Grand Canal.
   Set down on arrival
my four-wheeler bag
makes its own way
to the window.

The first night
   I sleep
then wake
to churning water
   the reverse
and forward thrust
of *vaporetti*
arriving   leaving the wharf.
   I nap
through the backwash
   the slap and drag
beneath my window.
   Roused yet again
by disembodied chants…

prossima fermata Accademia
  Ponte dell'Accademia…
I thrash and roll
  find myself
on the *pavimento*.

(ii) *pavimento musivo* – mosaic floor

Here on Murano, this glittery, glass-blown
morning finds me escaping the *fornace*
for something cooler. In the *Basilica dei Santi*

Maria e Donato, I'm still peering at floors,
wandering aisles in lop-sided fashion, my sight
blurred from the maze of mosaics. In the golden

dome above the altar, *Santa Maria* shimmers
and stares; warns me off with her out-stretched
hands, tapering fingers. Or is it the latecomer,

the dragon-slaying *San Donato* who's being
rebuffed? After a century of living alone
perhaps the relics of saint (and beast)

were distasteful at her altar, especially
of a man said to kill with holy spittle!
I leave her in peace and find the font, so old,

it uses its stairs as a crutch – easy to picture the
anxious families, squalling babies with thighs
of angels, the splash and ritual of christenings.

The font is filled now with a glass mosaic,
a pool of radiant light. I stare into its depths,
lambent, magnified, a kaleidoscope to infinity.

Is this a conceit for divine power
or must I still face the *fornace*?

(iii)

Punta della Dogana
Forgotten Dream, David Hammons

If an artist can transform a basketball hoop into
a crystal chandelier, what might be this 'dream'

hidden in the tower? I climb the last steps,
look up and find a wedding dress, hanging

from a beam – a vintage gown of ivory satin,
trimmed and edged with lace. A scalloped train

falls low at the back, revealing a frayed crêpe-
de-chine lining. Long, fitted sleeves are ruched

at the shoulder, the bodice ornate. Who held it
close, with all love's promise? Who let it go?

The gown stirs on an updraught, turns,
billows, the train lifting, floating behind.

Now the bride kicks out her skirts.
A mirrored echo, white light flickers and dazzles

through open windows. Below the tower, waters
of the Guidecca meet the Grand Canal, this prow-

shaped point, like a vessel, waiting at the city
entrance, the bride, its swaying figurehead.

The breeze subsides, the dress falls still,
secrets and dreams return to their folds.

(iv) *pavimentato cortile* – paved courtyard

A perfect night…*perfetto*…corner table…attentive waiters…
the first cool sip of Soave…*per favore* and *grazie* flowing like the
wine. But halfway through *il primo*, the mood was broken in the
same way a cough disrupts a concert hall. We heard them before
we saw them; a mid-life couple in matching T-shirts from Des
Moines, to be seated where we became unwilling eavesdroppers.
He removed his Lions cap and demanded translation of the
menu, at the same time complaining it was not the sort of
food he was used to back home in Iowa. Order placed, he set
up his iPad, then read to his wife (and the rest of us) all ten
of Someone's *Best Things To Do In Venice*. She said little but sat,
turning a wedding band round and around her finger. When
he reached number eight…*while extremely touristy and nothing
short of a major cliché, seeing the Grand Canal from the Rialto Bridge is
just something that everyone must do*…she let out an *Oh mah Lawd*,
and laughed in a nervy, high-pitched way. Watching her, I was
reminded of Rilke's angels: *They all have mouths so tired, tired…*
But her husband wasn't one to linger over his food. As they
were leaving, he slapped his cap back on his head, remarking
in somewhat baffled tones *Well, I couldn't complain about the fish.*

(v) *un ultimo a piedi* – a last walk

Remember the garden of the Guggenheim Palazzo,
a rare, green space beside the Canal? You wander
the paths among artless plantings, the well-bedded
sculptures; pause at her grave: *Peggy Guggenheim*,
        still here, with her dogs.

In a walled corner, a love poem is engraved
on a bench of Istrian stone. Sit for a while, let
your fingers scan the words, feel the cut
in the smooth, white surface but don't linger
at the line, *I AM LOSING TIME*.

Leave by a side-gate of ornate black iron, inset
with glass like a peacock's tail; follow the lane
between high brick walls and faded stucco, past
rows of doors with polished bells, turn a corner
and there you find it – the little piazza.

Like great-aunts watching over a child, the square
lives on through its central garden. Fine-leaved maples
filter the sky, briars of roses writhe and trail, a hooped-
iron railing edges the grass. From a side-canal comes
a splash of cyan and I'm sure, yes, there is – an age-old

fountain, a toothless lion dribbling water. You
rest in the shade, let it seep in; half-bright, half-dark
in the day's late light; the way a shutter folds back
on a wall; a door, half-open behind iron-lace;
exchanges of banter – the hands, the eyes!

Later, the sun will drop behind the lagoon, the skyline
turn to ink. Each way you look, lights will flare,
along the Zattere, across the Guidecca; pin-pointing
bridges and waterways, flooding all that is fantastical.
And this evening, like every other, the streets will fill,
      the *passeggiata*, about to begin.

Notes
(i) *pavimento* – floor; *vaporetti* – small passenger ferries; *prossima fermata* – next stop
(ii) *fornace* – furnace. The Venetian glass-blowing industry was moved to the island of Murano in the 13th century.
(iii) Punta della Dogana is a contemporary art centre in Venice's old customs building.
(v) *Panchina da Giardino* – Garden Bench 2001, Jenny Holzer, The Sculpture Garden of the Peggy Guggenheim Palazzo Venier dei Leoni; *passeggiata* – traditional evening stroll

family business

In the long mirror, I watch Stefano,
effusive, amiable working the floor.

Ciao bella, he waves, though his greeting
is lost in blasts from the dryers.

Black hair, black pants, black shirt; cuffs
folded high release his wrists as he combs

and cuts, spins on his chair. Along with the
patter he issues a flow of directives to staff.

Facing me in the gilded frame, Sophia pauses
to flick my fringe; perhaps she's caught me

watching him. With a hint of embarrassment,
or maybe awe, she shrugs and says, *my brother,*

you know, he sees everything! Sophia's never
been to Italy, has lost the few words she learned

from her Nonna. Dark-browed, dark-lashed,
dark-eyed, swathes of hair tipping

the cheekbones of her long, oval face –
pure Modigliani.

chiaroscuro

19th Century Master Drawings from the Prat Collection

The lights are subdued, the rooms, hushed
    only a murmur along the walls.
The Gallery guard shifts on his stool.

To stand so near these fragile drawings
is to glimpse the hand at work
with the bright and the dark
    to see light lift through shadow.

In fierce strokes of charcoal, Cezanne
shapes a head.   Seurat's careful hand
shades with black conté crayon.
        With pen and ink
Delacroix conjures skirmish.
Ingres draws his wife, a sonnet in pencil.

A poem may start this way, the words
still forming, thoughts unclear – a time
to press lightly, hold your breath.
As images come faster, pencil bolder,
    so with words.

Outside, the clouds hang low,
where blue jacaranda smudges the grey.

dancing figure

Auguste Rodin, 1905, graphite & watercolour

were it not for her hair, coiled
       and confined
she could be a naiad
       about to flee

light on one leg
       for a breathless moment
she leans forward   turns her head, lifts
       and folds an arm
       over her shoulder

in passing, a tendril of hair springs free

her hand reaches down
       for the toes
       the arcing foot
       and the leg, bent up behind her

when fingers brush toes she's fully extended
       her body held in one lithe movement

he brings us this moment
       with a skitter of pencil, a wash of paint

redhead (bathing) 1889

Henri de Toulouse-Lautrec

A small white back, somehow supplicant
beneath our gaze. She could be your daughter
or mine, seated on a rug, legs wide
her posture lewd, a touch defiant.

She seems so young; she could be your daughter
leaning forward, elbow resting on her knee
the posture lewd, a touch defiant;
one stocking half-rolled up, or down, her thigh,

leaning forward, elbow resting on a knee;
titillation in the scattered clothes, black
stocking half-rolled down, or up, her thigh.
We see her from behind, her shoulders bare,

titillation in the scattered clothes,
an undergarment loose about her hips.
He paints her from behind – the shadowed spine,
the hair, a flaming crown around her head,

an undergarment loose about her hips,
all secrets of her body barred from view.
The flaming weight of hair around her head
he captures in a chignon at the neck.

Her face, her private parts, he hides from view;
his model, seated on a rug, legs wide.
Across the room, we turn to look again –
her small white back, somehow supplicant.

torso, 1954

Jarrah wood, Rosemary Madigan

did she call you
   did she cry out for release?

or did you find her
buried in hardwood
   the red-dark heart of jarrah,
her skin alight with sapwood
   lithe with fiddleback

did you know
she would be so ripe?
   this is no young girl
with narrow hips, unyielding flesh –
   she's in her prime

her stance evokes deities
from temple caves
   a slight turn of waist
tightens buttocks, profiles
her breasts, contours the spine

how sure was your touch
as you hollowed her armpits
   outlined tendons
shaped the arc of her ribs

and as you searched
with knives and chisels
   rasps and rifflers
did she guide your hand

around the curve of her belly
the knot of her navel?

   by then were you working
woman to woman?

Eingana, 1968

Carved English limewood, horizontal relief, Rosemary Madigan

'It was the Aboriginal story, and I was reading those stories at the time… I haven't done anything like that before or since…my work doesn't have literary connections really…'

For its fine, light grain, she chooses limewood.
The timber is yellow, will turn to gold
as light invades the open relief. She can work
by hand, without hammer or mallet; each detail

from the myth, *Eingana*, the rainbow serpent,
pierced by a spear and from the wound
        all is created.
Her touch is sure, the limewood flows;

animals, a tree, sacred mountains rise in relief;
each attached to the writhing serpent, its swollen
belly ready to spill. And the spear must plunge deep –
        this is the moment before creation.

Her own story is different, yet so much, the same;
a love she'll combine. On one corner she carves
the hand of the father; near the tree, symbols
for bread and water. To Eingana she gives

the face of Mary; suggests a halo, gliding over
her head. On the left, a large and intricate ear,
both pinna and cochlea, (or is it a sea-snail)
entwined with the coils of the sweet-faced serpent.

There's one space left – a bird insists.
    Unsure, she waits, but the message is strong.

She carves a pelican
   and the bird belongs.
Elegant, slender, its long beak snapping,
from the yellow wood of the linden tree.

Ref.: James Gleeson Oral History Collection, NGA

forensic

'hey,… / push on/ nothing left to see here/ move along.' – alicia sometimes

(i) 1954 – *City Hotel room – 6 cellulose negatives*

Trousers, tightly folded, on a metal-rimmed
trunk; a patterned tie hung over the mirror.
Two combs, a notebook, the evening
news, spread in a row across the table.

In the wastepaper basket, something
screwed up   a bill?   letter?
        the only thing not friggin' neat
Your camera pauses: small

white handkerchief, edged with lace.
       Shift further right: alarm clock
stopped at 9.22; washbag, closed.
Two clean glasses on the marble stand,

thin grey towel on the basin rail.
Your eye, the camera, returns its sweep
to the single iron bed, candlewick
cover smoothed and straightened –

       windows flung wide,
curtains looped back. Outside
a canyon of buildings, blank-
walled, empty. You know

what you'll see when you move
to the sill, climb on a chair
and steady the street-shot –
       six floors down.

(ii)

The wife always knows when I've copped
a 'jumper'. *Bad day was it love?* She
stops cooking tea, herds the kids

out of the kitchen before my fuse blows,
gives me a look, hands me a beer.
The vegies could do with a bit of watering;

stacks of time if you'd like a breather.
She got it in one, hang on
so tight, forget to breathe; still

seeing that shot; him sprawled face down
in those striped pyjamas, could've been
sleeping, poor young bugger.

It's warm in the yard, might even rain;
      drag on a smoke, drain half a beer; curse
as something snaps beneath my boot –

dratted kids when'll they learn
to pick up their dolls? Light's going fast,
best time of all, set the hose to fine-spray

watch water play from side to side. Along
with the drenching, a tightness shifts; I
can smell herbs now, mint and thyme.

A screen door slams. Someone warm
and solid tackles my legs, throws me forward.
The wife's anxious face appears at the window;

I give her the nod that he's OK. *You gotta come
in Dad, wanna play horsies 'n' Mum says nearly
story time.* I turn off the hose and gather him up;

high on my shoulders, he shrieks with joy, sturdy
legs clamped round my neck, skin as smooth
as gold-top cream. I find his ankles, hold them

tight, wince as fingers grab my hair – sweet
from his bath, I breathe him in, his pulsing life
       his trust in me.

(iii)

later always later sometimes hours sometimes weeks first the
eye disembodied clicks open edge of dreamland never blinks
you're behind it in the frame too watcher and watched you
know it's a nightmare this is your local, remember but no six
o'clock closing for you mate it's on to the strip show the late late
sleaze light cones down sweeps and swings searchlights criss-
crossing tracking death-camp walls never know what you'll see
poor creature striped prison garb crawling away falls on his
face rolls over stares up baby-doll eyes china blue painted
lashes smashed cheeks mud on lace you're being shaken the
eye won't close someone's holding you *another bad dream love
you're OK it's only a dream love* the eye won't close *only a dream love
you're OK only a dream   a dream*

Suggested by archival photographs viewed at the NSW Justice and
Police Museum

vigilance

Suggested by untitled painting, 2008, Trudy Fennell

A small girl is poised
at the edge of the playground
        that first headlong rush
suddenly halted. One foot is lagging
behind in the grass – the next step will take her
deep into woodchips.

One arm is tucked close
like a folded wing. The other
raised, bent at the elbow
as if ready for flight.   Her head
is cocked, motionless.
But her eyes are everywhere.

Like you, wild bird, picking your way
through the margins of our lives; flicking
your tail to show snow-white coverts;
red legs strutting through reeds
and rushes; scarlet bill probing, plumage
melding into mauve-shadowed pools.

Swamphen, you show us the joy of colour,
remind us that watchers are watched.

In the Detail, a poetry competition, 2010, was organised by the
NSW Hunter Writers Centre – poems written to accompany various
artworks designed by students of Newcastle University.

a weight of hair

On hot days, you see girls doing it everywhere – by a fountain,
at a desk, sitting on a bus or under a tree. In languid sequence,

they lean forward, close their eyes, raise their arms, lift and hold
a load of hair from the neck then wait – maybe wait some more –

before they let it fall, heavy on the shoulders. Or they lift and twist,
fiddle with clips and bands, secure the coil high on their heads

so air can reach and cool. You saw it too when she sat up in bed,
drenched with fever; thumped and turned the pillow, arced back

to lift the sweat-dark hair from her face and cried *that's enough*.
Younger still, a hot tired child running towards you, how your

fingers eased beneath the collar to free the clinging strands.
You see a woman, sometimes serene, sometimes weary but

still there, head held high, and all you want to do
       is reach out and lift, like a memory,

the weight of her hair from the nape of her neck.

the music tower

Small, but insistent, like notes of complaint,
your crepe soles squeak across parquet floors.

Behind you, the voices from classrooms
fade. The corridor ends with a closed door.

When you're almost there, a new sound takes over,
a muted discord swells to a clamour

as you open the door on a flight of stairs. Piano
scales stumble from major to minor; violins

labour on poorly bowed strings; trombones
and trumpets blurt and blare. From upstairs rooms

come weary pleas, *try it one more time, dear…*
At the top step, you pause and ready yourself

to knock on the door where she'll be waiting;
a patient smile beneath rolls of blue hair,

red lipstick-lips transferred to her cup, tea
still steaming, Nice biscuit dissolving

in the saucer's slops. As you find your music,
she'll pat the piano-stool and suggest

a few scales *to warm up the fingers*. So
will start your weekly hour of humiliation.

But today, you can't face her unfailing restraint;
you don't want to listen to smothered sighs

or *Für Elise*, the way it would sound if
practised daily, with sight-reading too.

You drop your hand, amazed at such daring,
run from the tower and slam the door.

Small, but insistent, like quavers of conscience,
your soles squeak back along parquet floors.

flying blind

or riding tandem
for Robert

(i)

Like a water diviner
       his long cane the sensor
he reads new terrain
to find safe passage.

On the bush-track, flickering
sunlight spreads deception
       is the path filled with shadows
or deep black holes?

He follows the boots
of the one before him
       if they disappear
which way should he turn?

(ii)

He tells me
he'll ride tandem tomorrow.

There's an edge to his voice
       but he grins.

       I hear
a white cane snapping –

see two men lean as one
and set the wheels spinning.

dry spell

The rain came overnight, cat-like at first, stealthy
on tiles, careful over gutters. By morning, she knew
the dry-spell was over; ran a bath to celebrate.

Steam rose, mirrors misted, all was slippery,
steeped in rainsong, spilling into pipes and tanks,
soaking the earth. Deep in bathwater, behind

closed lids, she moved through her garden; lilly
pilly, acacia, grevillea, tossed in the drenching;
      the lorikeets upside-down with joy.

Almost submerged, she followed the labyrinth
of roots; traced each fibre writhing, reaching
into fertile soil. She wriggled her toes, sank deeper.

Words and images came bubbling to the surface, tipped
over enjambments, pooled in reflection, flowed on.
      As the rain eased, she reached for a pen.

3

'We write in an echo chamber…'
Maria Takolander

the Green Room

for Deb

In the Writers' House, we are granted seclusion.
We open and close doors quietly; tiptoe
through landscapes, rich in metaphor; wait
till nightfall to mingle, light fires.

Behind the house, a stand of old pines
is under sentence. The felling starts early. All day,
words are mocked by chainsaws, thoughts truncated,
nerves exposed. We wince with the juddering earth.

By late afternoon a bleeping crescendo signals
the end; revving engines falter, fade.
       In the sudden stillness, relief expands but
all at once, like noise replacements

called up from the rear, two helicopters
beat their way across the sky. Backwards
and forwards they track, then drop
into the valley, spinning apprehension.

In the garden, natural order returns.
Butcher birds and magpies hurtle through the air,
defiant calls scrambling, like the rhododendrons,
high into the canopy. A neighbouring dog

yelps and retires. From my first-floor window
I watch wisteria bullying crab-apple; through
the other, the falling sun. On my desk,
white paper, black pen, a sharpened pencil;

in the Green Room, cornered.

pile high the platter – the mint is free

the dictator of the ear is sensual
       so move somnambulist   move

your quotidian   the hex
       of lyric arousal

don't scratch the angst
       embrace the turmoil

stir   the creative
visit carnevale

and when the tempo tells you
you're light-filled   layered

roll the dice and gasp *frivolous*

funambulism

you are a highwire   s t r u n g
  between rooftops
      i am the stuntman
  crossing at dawn

you are the skin   s t r e t c h e d
  over a djembé
      mine are the fingers
  that call up your voices

you are a reed-bed   b o w e d
  by the river
      the surge of my tides
  lifts you to dance

you are a rock face   s h e e r
  to the ocean
      i am the abseiler
  swaying before you

you are a powerline   h a u n t e d
  by wind
      we are the silence
  that follows a storm

the gift

white linen on the tray
tea and toast   a single rose

i could see he was excited
his hands were shaking   those slim

brown fingers, silent marauders of sleep
i smiled and took the tray, spilt

the tea (clumsy me)   a small tic
flicked by his lips; he disappeared

came back with a package, wrapped
and tied, now i was trembling

well go on he said
settling beside me on the bed

i untied the ribbon, peeled off gold seals
eased back tissue, layer on layer

until my fingers found two half-moon mounds
of foam, strung together on a single cord

not the expected piece of lingerie but
a sea-green bikini   *go on, try it on*

he urged then laughed, bragged how
he'd used his hands to show my size

i arranged it on our bed

the padded top, side-tied bottoms

and there she lay between us
    her full breasts cupped to perfection

her navel, glinting from an oiled
and sun-tanned belly

    beneath last year's negligée
my small white breasts froze

levitation with LBD

i used to wear it to walk on air
        black crepe falling from a satin yoke

i used to wear it to change my spots
        black satin cuffs caught at the wrist

i used to wear it to escape the bored room
        black silhouette against crisp white linen

to dance with the prince i used to wear it
        black silk underslip close to my skin

to up the ante i used to wear it
        jet black buttons looped at the neck

to play with fire i used to wear it
        little black wraith like smoke in my mind

sliced lime

he sits facing her
                across the table

everything about him
                a little slacker now

from the wine   the food
                the effort of charm

she knows
                he thinks   it's on

she knows
                it's not

after the door is closed
        after the angry revs of a car
              the night resumes its silence

into a shallow white dish
        she tosses
              the remnants of their feast

where they nudge to rest
        in an intimacy
              of oils

a sliced green lime
        cast aside

quiet carriage

'quiet carriages are customer regulated' – CountryRail NSW website

no gossip   no ring-tones   no blare
but somewhere behind me
a man starts snoring
       ugly strangled sounds
as though he's dying

across the aisle
a young kid sprawls
       eyes-closed-legs-twitching-brain-wired
i covet his headset
       his state of oblivion

a rabbit's running beside the track
       it stops
            looks around
disappears into the bush
with a hint of white tail

the irony
       makes me grin
out there   free
me in here
planning the perfect crime

shock waves

our paths cross
        most mornings

i'm on my walk by the bay
he's off to high school

our eyes never meet
        he studies the ground
or stares into space

probably surfing
        a wave   or the net
planning neat moves
        for *assassin's creed*

someone's made sure his shirt
is clean though half the buttons
are undone   his shorts
are sliding off his hips   he's
holding a tie and shoes in one hand
        the other controls
a bag that drags from his shoulder

on Shakespeare's 'stage'   he's heading up
        i'm in decline   yet
each time we pass something's
familiar   perhaps it's the gait

one day as usual   i see him approaching
        hair sculpted
        expression vague
as we pass   a certain aroma

swirls on the breeze   YES   that's it
the Age of Product has closed
the gap – we both style our hair
with *ExTReme ShoCK-WavE* gel

Lord Howe Island

The way the clouds keep
pulling away but always
return to the mountains;

how the surf breaks free
of the coral reef to run back
over crushed white sand.

And those corpulent fish that wallow
and thrash till you wade through
the shallows to feed them.

There's a shiftiness here…

Before first light, it's doves
and pigeons to croon you awake, like
dreams of an English childhood;

and who could believe amongst
tropical palms to hear
blackbirds sing *appassionati*?

In the glass-bottomed boat
we lurch   and bob   and wait
for the giant turtles. I wonder

if Eve had the same unease
or was just tired of perfection.

spectral horizon

Gulf-Savannah notebook

Darwin to Burketown

Darwin at midnight
anticipation
laden with baggage

ceiling-fan shudders
Bushell's tea bags
hi-way motel

bougainvillea
through tinted windows
winter is summer

Adelaide River
lawn perspective
aisles of young bones

lilac and lavender
plants to soothe sleep
honour the dead

under canvas
bird calls at dawn
unzip the sky

Mataranka
peacocks strolling
outside my tent

cabbage tree palms
thermal pools steam
fruit bats rampage

flashes of yellow
between tufts of spinifex
kapok glimpses

termite cemeteries
monumental sculptures
underground toil

white water slides
over the causeway
at Roper Bar

home is a tent
pack and repack
fold and unfold

named Cape Crawford
canyons of sandstone
miles from the ocean

beside the road
bustards flap, black kites wheel
flights of doves

Heartbreak Hotel
doesn't pamper its guests
sorry mate she says

amenities closed –
young man with dreadlocks
the stink of red mud

long day's drive
slowed by dry creek-beds
chattering fades

out of Burketown
brolgas on grassland
unbroken horizon

mysterious roll cloud
from over the ocean
Morning Glory

Burketown pub
ravaged by fire
spectral horizon

gliding the Glories

Never a boom town, Burketown, though history shows
it tried. But once a year for weeks before the wet,
the township sweats and swells with glider and
hang-glider pilots, with nature photographers

needing a scoop, with tribes of grey nomads,
curious tourists and anyone else who's
picked up the vibe. You can tell by their eyes
if they've seen one before, they glow like a croc's

trapped in flashlight, you can tell by the yarns
they love to share, of those years when they waited,
but not in vain, when the Morning Glories came
rolling through town. *Imagine* they say *waiting*

at dawn, like every day, watching the horizon,
yawning, staring   you blink again and this cloud
appears   this fan-bloody-tastic unbroken cloud
that stretches right across the Gulf   rolls towards

shore like a surfer's dream   most times there's one
but sometimes there's rows of 'em, rolling behind.
And mate, if you make it, you cannot imagine
what it's like being up there, gliding a Glory.

The hopefuls sigh, sweat some more in the round
forty heat, stare in their beers as weeks disappear
and the wet season looms. *They call 'em roll clouds,*
driven by wind   move up to 60 ks an hour

can be a thousand kilometres long   one to two
ks high   a hundred metres above your head.
Sometimes there's shapes, like you get
in ice, a feather, a bear, a roaring dragon.

Icarus-like in their wind-sheared cloud,
the golden ones surf the sky, flirt with sunrise,
cruise to the coast. With rising heat, the cloud
breaks up. Dream ride over, they plunge to the plains.

When fridges frosted over at the Burketown
Pub (before a fire destroyed it last year,)
the locals would tell you to set your alarm
and prepare for a Glory arriving at dawn.

With the wet coming in
    and the old pub gone,
only its memory
        disturbs the horizon.

a re-write

the pencil cuts deep
        outside, a barking owl
coughs up choked memories; truth

is a precious metal
        only mallets and hammers
can fashion its curves

searching through the night
        words against the stars
burnished into gleaming

sound bite

it wasn't anything he said
  or any way he looked
    it wasn't the truth
      that we never got near

      it was just the way he whistled
    as he came through a door
  that left me
undone

pendulous wattle

'I have grown learnèd in sorrow.' – Li Ch'ing-Chao (c.1084–c.1151)

'Your joy is your sorrow unmasked.' – Khalil Gibran, 1923

To your soil I bring remnants, mulch
you with memories; in autumn, rich
castings and potions from worms.

All winter you tremble. Rain clings
to your leaves, sticky and dense; you shake it
away. Each spring, hang low, weighed down

with the future, a golden promise already
in bloom. Through summer, sea-breezes
swirl under your branches, lifting them high.

Still you struggle; rising, falling;
but it's your habit of falling that tips
the scales between sorrow and joy.

well-bred

Black muzzle resting between your forepaws,
> you spread yourself like a fleece
across the carpet.

As I glance through the doorway
I can hear her breathing, in gentle snores
that flutter the tissues she's tucked
in her glasses, against afternoon glare.

You roll one eye in my direction
as though to remind me that you're
on duty, you're always on duty
through the slow, silent hours
she spends here alone.

She bred you herself. You are her
black boy, you danced on hind legs. You
brought her trophies, *Best of the Breed.*
The others long gone, *hard work, the
bitches,* those years of fine show-work
now ribbon-filled drawers.

Before he vanished, you'd escape
downstairs and sit while his fingers
probed your jaw. He'd take you
outside and tease you with sticks
till you'd run like a mad thing,
bursting with life.

You'd doze at his feet through
the rambling stories, but as he grew
weaker, he kept insisting that you
must stay with her, be good
and stay with her, for soon they
would come and take him away.

the third bridge

for my mother

It was a clean, sharp day
      cut through with winds
from the Southern Ocean, so we wrapped
her in rugs and pushed the wheelchair
along the boardwalk, through rushes
and reed beds, the grieving swans
the calling, circling terns.

At the third bridge, we stopped.
      Beneath us, a tidal high,
the wind-dragged, surging estuary,
its sun-flecked surface.
And there we took turns to toss
him over – handful by handful,
back to the river, back to the ocean.

But caught at first
on gusts of wind, his ashes
      lifted against the light
then circled and swirled in exultant loops
before the final fall –
the quiet passage beneath the bridge.

beyond my mother's garden

for my sisters

Friday

Grey sky.   Sunrise, a smudge of red, a lipstick smear.
The last tendrils of fog cling to the river. In her garden,
autumn's work is almost done

Today, she's calm. Since leaving home, that sharp mind has flown the coop. Now we travel continents in seconds, attribute unfamiliar sweetness to old enemies, find no grounds for sparring. Oh! we have railed, she and I, stubborn genes never back down, but I'm waved away – sleep is all she craves.

Saturday

Late start. Sun full pelt on my morning face. Too late for the river's waking insights;   no layers, no swathes of fog; no eerie lights travelling the far bank. It's strangely warm, I'll take in the last of her roses.

The quiet days have fled. It's warfare now…full frontal, the near-blind eyes glare into a tormented world. Every ploy I take returns us to evil; it lurks in corridors, waits behind bathroom doors, is brewing in kitchens, withholding drugs.

Sunday

Last night, hidden behind velvet, a full white moon, large and low. Between us, so black, the ghost-gum silhouette.

At the open door, I watch and wait, hoping for change. But still she glares; unseeing eyes fixed on dark troubled spaces. All night I fret, mind as crazed as hers; her shrinking body stranded, clawed hands clutching my arm, spasms of choking…

Monday

Frost, melting fast in early sun. Low tide, the mud flats pooled and draining, splashes of blue sky. A sparrow lands on the deck, wary, watchful, as if waiting for the usual roars. I'm as flat as the river.

She's being moved into a 'princess' chair for a trial. I don't think they realise she's always been the queen.

Tuesday

Smothering cloud, low, quilted; the river, a mean streak. Only the sparrows have some cheek. The last yellow leaves cling before release, the downward spiral.

She was out of her room, lined up in her chair among a parody of sun-loungers. Mush was being spooned into her mouth. She spat it out as the man next to her coughed up phlegm. She mouthed to me 'I want to die.'

Wednesday

Dense fog smothering the garden. The tip of the silver birch, my mast-head and horizon. Later, a watery sun brings a shifting, smoking haze; roof-line surfaces, a floating chimney, everything coming back into perspective.

After my concerns, requests, I find her tucked in, dozing, happy. 'They haven't tortured me yet today' she says. I pat her hand, watch her sleep, then run away – hold this quiet image throughout the day as I go through her drawers like a thief, beginning to sort the garnering of years.

Thursday

Rain is forecast. Black clouds mass and rise to form peaks and valleys. Wisps of white cirrus sail across the darkness. A light-scalloped rim appears, spreads. In moments, the sun bursts through, the clouds disperse. It might never have been.

We are all agreed – no more rides in princess chairs, no leaving her room, no pretence of better days to come.

Friday

Thin strands of fog; autumn's last day. The river is layered like cloud, merges, disappears. Black wings flit through the trees. A flock of white corellas broods on the playing-field. A chimney-stack smokes into the sky.

She trusts her carers now, stops fighting. One day, her eyelids flicker, stay closed. Every breath takes her deeper, deep into her own peace. She squeezes our hands. She knows we are there.

new day

an edge of sand around the bay
        a line of surf across the bar
                against the wall, a surge of tide
a hint of sun on a distant lighthouse

bright yellow buoys mark out the channel
        a solitary cormorant dives for fish
                clinking at anchor, five white yachts
red-legged gulls silver the shallows

beyond Barrenjoey the horizon blurs
        almost a memory, last night's moon
                a sea-eagle crosses the path of the sun
Lion Island, released from mist.

Gillian Telford has been writing poetry since moving from Sydney to the NSW Central Coast in the 1990s, with work published regularly in journals, anthologies and online sites. Longer poem sequences have twice been shortlisted for the Newcastle Poetry Prize. She was an active member of Central Coast Poets Inc. for over ten years, and during that time co-edited three of their biennial Henry Kendall Award anthologies. In 2009 she guest-edited the Tasmanian magazine *Prospect*, and in 2010 was invited to work with choreographer Françoise Angenieux and composer Solange Kershaw in the collaboration *Poetica, Five Arrivals*, a Gosford City Council/Sydney Writers' Festival regional event.

The poems in *An Indrawn Breath* have been selected from work written since her first collection was published in 2008.

www.ingramcontent.com/pod-product-compliance
Lightning Source LLC
Chambersburg PA
CBHW071024080526
44587CB00015B/2481